Here
is a
beginning

Jo O'Farrell

HB

Published by Honeybee Books
Broadoak, Dorset
www.honeybeebooks.co.uk

Printed in the UK using paper from sustainable sources

ISBN: 978-1-910616-37-6

The Living Tree

Living well with and beyond cancer

All proceeds from this book go to the The Living Tree self-help support group for people who have experienced cancer and for their families/carers.
www.thelivingtree.org.uk

Thank you to Louise Ramsden and Ros Cole for their help in editing and proof reading.

To Vince
with all my love

Introduction

I had been writing poems occasionally for some years when I came across David Adam's compilation Borderlands. He was at that time Vicar of Lindisfarne and wrote books, prayers and poems in the Celtic Christian tradition. His writings inspired me and I began to write more poetry more often.

Then six years ago I became ill and was diagnosed with non-Hodgkin lymphoma, a blood cancer, and my life changed forever. Though there were times when I couldn't write at all, writing has provided a cathartic outlet for my fears, anger, grief – the gamut of emotions that come with a cancer diagnosis and the treatment that follows. As I say in "I didn't know", I now had a reason to write.

In 2012, through Rosie Jackson and her cancer writing workshops, I met Jo Millar and The Living Tree was born. We both felt the need for a local group to support people in living well with and post cancer. It is difficult to express how important The Living Tree has become in my life, how much it means to so many of us involved in it – the amazing people we have met, the new activities we have tried, the sorrows and joys we have shared, the pain and laughter. Such support is beyond price.

I travel this cancer journey alongside my husband, Vince, the standing stone I lean against through every vicissitude, for better or worse as he vowed 42 years ago. My lovely daughters Elizabeth (cover artist) and Caitlin keep me smiling and grounded. And a myriad of friends continue to support me with their thoughtfulness and constant prayers, holding me in the Light.

I really appreciate the kind words Rosie and Margie have written for this book. Rosie has been a constant source of advice and encouragement with my writing.

Take a workshop with her if you can: www.rosiejackson.org.uk

Cancer has opened many doors for me and showered me with unexpected blessings. I have learned that as each new day dawns, 'here is a beginning...'

Contents

Before

After

Before

Tea dance

Beneath skirts
of rippling silk
iridescent blue
garment for saint
or seer or you

briny lace it comes
foaming tumbling
cappuccino froth
of pristine petticoat
which retreating
trails its traces like
a ragged hemline rent

bequeathing
intricate patterns
of woven white filigree
to the shore

The main man

definitely David
a desert sheik
that's made it
leaving us
a legacy of praise
obstinately human
will he ever learn his lesson
promising to serve you all his days

creditably kingly
a major player singly
in the annals of the Hebrew nation
proving if he had to
he's not the country hick who
bumped off in solo style the opposition

never less than shepherd
his whole lifetime coloured
by a love of God beyond all measure
next time I feel jaded
I'll meditate on David
and sing his psalms full of gold to treasure

Garden song

I do not know
the green of it
that shades along
the borders over lawn,
though you can
name a colour
for each plant
and blade of grass

I do not know
the scent of it
that fills my garden
through the book of hours
though you breathe
bouquets
of every fragrance
on the wind

I do not know
the dance of it that blows
the filigree of patterns
shadowing my feet,
though you
who call the tune
can name each
movement

I do not know
the taste of it
crisp to the teeth
or subtly on my tongue,
though you who
grew the orchard
know every fruit

so I will be determined
study hard the scriptures
of the soil
until I do
know
you

Eurythmic

Peace stole up on me
in that waiting room
between strife and disorder
an oasis space
to lick my wounds
rest and regroup

Eyes closed, freedom
at last to be
no longer a collection
of disparate parts
but a concord of
melodious sound
whole and complete

Let the world mirror love
and cease
its turmoil
grasp armistice moments
gain in the ensuing rush
the symmetry for which
we are created

Meanwhile I am learning
not to rail and lament
but gather my anger
and tears into tranquility
practice a ministry
of harmonious presence
on this discordant earth.

Grace

amongst the gravestones
she came out to play
through grasses gently stirring
birdsong and tree sway sounding
only the silent watcher sitting
saw her pass
delicate upon the green and lush
flowers wild in her eyes
and breeze upon her lips
stepping so lightly
through the veil

always she keeps her tryst
if you but rest awhile
and gently wait

After the storm

When lightning
strikes
startling illumination
and in
the bright white light

sometimes angels
gently waiting
to see
if I'm still here

sometimes a word
a phrase
turbulence disturbing
my comfort zone

the pages of a book
whip up a wind
to breathe me deep
of revelation rising

sometimes a poem
creeps around
my heart
catching me unawares

a tree, a flower
alive with love
sings to my surly soul
Creation's song

sometimes a look
a touch
rings resurrection
in my ears
grown deaf to silence

Then I am struck
again
illuminated
by lightning's
bright white
Light

Dwelling place

If it is true
I should be
different
carry an aura
an epiphany
of gold
jewel bright colours
embroidered angels
in my holiness
if it is true

If it is true
it is my task
to build
this sanctuary
not somewhere
outside
to visit when
I have the time
but here
within
where there's
no escape
if it is true

If it is true
then I must
reverence
myself
and her
and him
and see
the glory
even when
lost beneath
the grime
if it is true

If it is true
these tears
I shed
are blessings
holy as
any water
in a church
an offering
a gift
of love
if it is true

If it is true
try as I may
to put out
the light
clear the table
take down
the altar
turn away
the dwelling place
remains

Blessed bees

breakfasted
chores left undone
brown boots
barging through
fast-fading bluebells
burgeoning bracken
startled young buck
bursting from trees

rest here for a drink
I think
browsing in birdsong
breeze playing lightly
over boats becalmed
beneath blue haze
hill brow ablaze
with buttercups

banana time I think
blithe blanched butterflies
by beacon bold
buxom beasts
gently swishing tails
beneath the blossom
jaunty jays
blue flash flying

brook bubbling over
buried boulders
bleached beach brink
to briny water
toes dipped to cool
before best foot forward
back

earth and sky a-buzz
with insect sound
beetles battling
bees busy abroad
beauty beyond belief
breath taking

Truth

I often wonder
when asked for my opinion
if truth is worth
the chasm it creates
so sensitised are we
to every nuance
of possible offence

Diplomacy might be
the better path
to keep the peace
prevent our fragile
egos shredding
on the jagged
rocks exposed

At turn of tide
small coracles of faith
can put across
or reaching hands
as differing perception
fortunately fails
to match our own

What is truth
Pilate said
perplexed
as it splintered wood

Myanmar gems

sun glints on rock
ruby rich
blood red

fear in the jungle
stepping over
deadly earth

whirling wind rush
through rice fields
destroying

on the gun barrel
a bush lark
singing

flames on horizon
smoke rising
homeless

at border crossing
the gentle whir
of bees' wings

ripples in the stream
child's fragile touch
remembering

prayers at sunset
counting beads
of hope

Herb garden

She planted each
with care
in shady nooks
where time would bring the sun
some grew tall and feathery
in endless shades
of green
or tinge of blue
others grew broad, compact
or crept along the paths

Sweet scent
or bitter gall
for balm or tincture
cooking pot or tea
fragrance for free
I never knew
all their purposes

But she did
and tended each
with love
for all had healing
in their touch
to ease our pain

Trust

Above the far horizon
where earth meets heaven
serried ranks of angels
cloud shaped hover
whilst the Creator's
great light shimmers
on the sea
and we
like pebbles on the beach
all colours
shapes and sizes
are held secure
in the enfolding Love
which sweeps around
the bay.

Weaving

Warp and weft
you weave
into the very fabric
of our lives.

Into the tapestry of hours
your shining strands flow
illumining the dullest day
the darkest night.

Nor may we disentangle
the precious thread
without unravelling
ourselves.

Closely firmly
lovingly
you hold all
together.

And the angels sang for Him

Bright blonde heads
often chosen
for angels
or fairies
nervously
they sang
and played
their parts
to much applause.

Often dismissive
me
of trees and tinsel
parties, presents,
childrens' plays
meaning lost.

But she
would have watched
with wonder
festive joy
clapped
at clever turns
eyes bright, heart proud
as he recited
from the Torah
for her

Why then
should I
be ashamed
of tears

Gilded flowers

Lost in her fragrant world
of greenery and growth
she doesn't hear
the footsteps in the nave
the admiration voiced
in whispered tones
as she creates
a psalmody of shape and colour
to delight the eye
and soothe the senses

Critical in survey
she muses on the gulf
'twixt plan and execution
sucking the thorn-pricked thumb
that placed the crimson rose
whilst silently we kneel
heads bowed
before her living story
his blood still dripping
from a tree

Time management

Like a roller coaster ride
I hurtled through
the week
crashed into Saturday
with streaming nose
and aching head
to pass a sleepless night.

Stop.
Switch off.
Close the diary.

close by your side
a safety pass
through crowds
of tasks and deadlines

touching your hem
a healing power
to change, create
alternative agenda

safe in your hands
raised up above
oceans of trivia
and diversions

Turn the page
a new day
dawns

Lupus

Name it
shame it
the wolf within
fanged fear inside
I dare to defeat
the dark
I name you

Claim it
tame it
the wolf within
pent pain inside
I hold my hope
on high
I claim you

Know it
show it
the wolf within
toothed tears inside
I choose to channel
change
I know you

Stop it
drop it
the wolf within
manged mask inside
I rip it roughly
to reveal
I stop you

Name it
disclaim it
the wolf within
hollow howls inside
I call Creator
take my chaos
I name you

for you have named me

(after Francis of Assisi)

Boxes

I wanted to make
everyone a box
the only practical thing
I'm any good at
and even then
some are a funny shape

but making boxes
is a bit noisy
for a quiet day
what are they for
you wonder and
sometimes so do I

but then again
you can put many
things into a box
poems and dreams
memories and take them
out to view

on dull days
or lonely nights
when time hangs heavy
or eyes are bright
with tears
better still

fill it
with chocolates
to entice you
with fragrant aromas
of exotic places
they wouldn't last long

in my box
so please accept
an imaginary box
filled with blessings
to hold your
very self

Screaming inside

Within these walls
marsh deep
in mire
struggling
sinking further

Call on me
you said
and caught
my cries

Solitary
mist wrapped
grasping
at crutches
slipping away

Lean on me
you said
and held
my heart

Cocooned
in icy fear
one step
a risk
too far

Rest in me
you said
and stroked
my soul

Climbing out
hazy light
numbness warmed
wetlands dried
pain pierced

Hazard with me
you said
dawning
deep

Looking back

I remember, I remember
the breakfasts that I've had
soggy cornflakes, sour milk
thanks a million Dad

I remember, I remember
the porridge in the pan
the syrup and the sugar
and sometimes even jam

I remember, I remember
the toasting lottery
overdone or underdone
which one will it be

I remember, I remember
the smell of sizzling lard
lion eggs with runny yolks
but much more likely hard

I remember, I remember
bacon on a Sunday
black pudding, sausages, fried bread -
and nothing left for Monday

Hey Moses

I admire your patience
and commitment
good humour
in the face of dingbats
with gentle calm
and the occasional roar
you stay alongside
this motley moaning
collection of
alternating
saints and sinners

I say straight up
no way
could I do this
endless journeying
with unkindred spirits
ditching my gems
of wisdom
every time I turn my back
to climb a mountain
or light up
a bush

I freely admit
to knowing others
who wear your sandals
managing their crews
with keen eye
and steady hand
full-voiced love
and open arms
forever taking one step more
to reach
the renegades

I acknowledge
the common thread
shekinah
community
in all your stories
somewhat reluctantly
I recognise
it must be my story
too

Spring

Turning the corner
I was surprised
caught off guard
by wayside primroses
quietly nestling
beneath the wall
adorning the path
heads held high
to greet the morning sun
and the passer-by.

A basketful of blessings
not to be picked
but left alone
to whisper praises
in gentle homage
to the giver of life.

For Vince

Whitsun

Flames
in the desert
conflagration
on the mountain
eyes shielded
knees bent
before awesome
power.

Dancing tongues
in an upper room
searing touch
courage ignited
mission ablaze
to teach
the Way.

Deep within
leaping light
flaring furnace
blazing beacon
swirling smoke
moves the
incandescent Spirit.

Refining love
pure gold
in the glowing embers
of the day.

After

The Saddest Thing

I might have passed
without knowing
over the cancer-curved horizon
ignorant of who I am

that would have been the saddest thing

within this damaged shell
open to life, love, loss
grows something priceless
that pearl
is me

A Poole of contrasts

Sunlight glints on shiny hulls
and Elekta 2 sparkles

sails flash along the horizon
light sears closed eyelids

houses nestle the shoreline
arms around my head ache

wind blows across the bay
shivers breeze over my flesh

rest on a warm bench
metal slab cold and unyielding

heat on my sky-turned face
healing rays burning deep

Poole without, Poole within
A pool of contrasts

(after radiotherapy)

Contemplating me

Who am I
this body
moving skeleton
clothed in water
elements
what we call flesh

I thought I knew
for all these years
of growth and change
of walk and talk
of children born
and parents gone
I thought I knew

until the day
I caught my breath
and fluid drained
and I lay face to face
with death

and then I knew
that I was something
more than this
much deeper
far beyond
the sentence passed
the words or pain

and I can be that me
despite the shadows
on the screen
live my life
inside the silence
know well
the path within
this moment's goal

Oh God, is this then
my soul?

Early rising

Here is an ending
I thought gazing
through window framing
hill green house brown
sky blues and other hues
sun-touched
frost-tipped
remote

dull days and sad stories
hot anger and iced fear
shadow creeping pain
per ardua ad astra
stardust and birdsong
world awakening warm
music in the wind

gently the patchwork mantle of my life
settles over my
shaking soul

Here is a beginning
I thought ...

Beyond the door

Pain shimmering
around the blurred edges
of my being
outside life moves on
a world I cannot reach
darkness envelops all
except the light
beyond the door

Smothering velvet
shades of gloomy grey
a swirling mist
of fear, frustration
isolating this small me
held by so many
in the light
beyond the door

Gifts tangible, nebulous
laughter, touch,
thoughts, words, prayers
pierce the numbness
ache of loss
beckon onwards
into the Light
beyond the open door

Dexterity

Men have never been
my favourite sex
women always seeming
more perceptive
and yet you came as he
though being
so much she
in all you said and did
so it seems fine
to hold your hands
feel safe and loved
within them
long delicate
but oh so strong
to keep so much
from falling

And I have
closed my eyes
and clung to them
on tricky cliffs
and slippy paths
in desperate places
on the very brink
and you have calmly
caught my aimless
fingers in your firm
but gentle grasp

weak, tired and aching
I rest now in those palms
knowing that all shall be well
all manner of things
shall be well

(after Julian of Norwich)

Aftermath

feeling the cold
no matter what the season
creeping round my neck
numbing fingers
legs bared no more
no naked arms
no lasting warmth

feeling panic rising
spilling over
tensed muscles, gut
cracked core
noisy crowds
busy places
anxiety reigns

feeling fatigue
tiredness that swoops
uninvited
eyes closing
unexpectedly
head drooping over
food and conversation

warm scarves
hats and layers
siestas
hardly reach
the edges

The cutting edge

Sometimes I'm sharp
of tongue
often he says
which makes me regretful
tearful even
It's not a new phenomenon
I can't blame it
on the illness,
it's an old dis-ease
it happens when I'm tired, frustrated
hungry, in a hurry
under stress

I should know better now
now that I have
a reason to be
sharp of tongue,
always I hope
my past frailties
will be overcome transformed
by the new strategies I've learned
to live well by

But the bristles
of the old me
still protrude

Touchstone

Her hand moved so fast
across the page
words spilling out
like seed scattered
across snow
to feed us

she sketched
children nestling
on her aching bones
entwined enshrined
in her sinews
and her soul

then luminous
through her pain
she smiled
her slender form
stilled, willed
at last to rest

courage flaming
she spoke
of love and loss
relinquishing
her essence to
a memory box

so briefly met and yet
just time to capture
that sweet laugh
a touch, some tears
to hold fast thro
the silent years

in memory of Lucy

Long song

A leaflet
at the chemo unit
told me
music could be
a great help
to recovery

music to suit your mood
it said
I read relax
to a delicate air
or a Taize prayer
and forget
your lack of hair

so I closed my eyes
to Brahms lullabies
put up my feet
to Debussy's beat
drifted off
to Tchaikov
sky

as brighter morns
overcome the grey
I board the Deadwood Stage
with Doris Day
Dance the Night Away
with Mavericks
or swing along
to a Glen Miller song

now I've settled down
to a gentler sound
along with Aled Jones
I've a Reason to Believe
a reprieve
from ills and pills
so take advice
All Angels can harmonise
you Into Paradise
absorb David Ferrard's
lilting bard

"Truly to sing,
that is a different breath"
said Rilke
whilst Eliot mused
"You are the music
while the music lasts"
but my simple
Abba acoustic is
Thank you for the Music

Small steps

I walked five miles
today or was it six?
forcing knees
stiff from sitting
and old age
up cliff paths
down rocky routes
muscles lazy from
drugs and drowsiness

but oh the joy of it
sheer sense of
achievement
of these small steps
to freedom
at last to venture
beyond
the safe and easy
routes

to soak in
the autumn sun
the salt tanged air
bathed in the sound
of sea and surf
on pebbles far from home

there will be a point
I know
beyond which I cannot
go
a step too far
but for now
five miles is enough
– or was it six?

Another Trolley Song

I'm a trolley dolly
its wheels are my best friends
I trundle down the corridor
and stroll from end to end

I'm a trolley dolly
like twins who've just been hatched
with valves and clips, lumens and lines
we're very much attached

The birth was quite traumatic
with cuts to set skin free
a Hickman line inserted
bonding my trolley and me

We always sleep together
it never leaves my side
such kindness and devotion
it fills us both with pride

My trolley feeds me daily
with stuff to keep me well
(that's if it doesn't kill me
and only time will tell!)

So I'm a trolley dolly
for three more days at least
then we'll divorce and I'll go home
from famine to a feast

I Didn't Know

I always knew I loved to walk
the hills above the sea
the paths around the shoreline
the ridge from here to there
the openness
the space

But I didn't know I loved
being able to walk
to put one foot before another
to achieve a few yards
climb a small hill
reach the crest
breathless

to look back, look down
and see what I'd achieved
to breathe freely again
no longer imprisoned
behind glass

I always knew I loved to write
but I didn't know I loved
having something at last
to say

(with thanks to Linda Pastan's
Things I Didn't Know I Loved)

Celebrate

I turn my blessings
love and yet more love
like photographs
of husband, daughters
grandchildren
into the light of living
I celebrate today
the here and now
that wraps me
warm and safe
from loneliness
and wasteful fears

I turn my blessings
smiles and laughter
like photographs
of friends strong
and resilient
into the light of living
I celebrate the words
and hugs
that wrap me
warm and safe
from sadness
and the empty space

I turn my blessings
faith and hope
like photographs
of me walking
striding unfettered
into the light of living
I celebrate moving
through landscapes
seascapes
wrapping me warm and safe
in the cradle
of creation

New Beginnings

she brought in a tray
of primula
bright hued amidst the green
you can choose one to paint
she said
so I choose deep purple velvet
delicate yellow centred
each petal's like a heart
she said
and I look as if for
the first time ever
and it is
so I begin to draw
the outlines
of a plant I thought I knew
but had never seen before
until today
how do others see me
I thought
what shape am I
since my map
has been re-drawn
my colours dimmed
my sheen rubbed off
still blooming
though in another hue

The Stranger

I didn't invite you in
but you came anyway
invading my spaces

You made yourself at home
spreading your possessions
in my fragile frame

Persistent repair work
drove you away
for a while

Too soon you were back
searching for nooks and crannies
to make your own

What's so special about me
to make you stop and stay
hang up your hat?

We've learned to rub along
avoid eye contact
too much conversation

Love calls me to hospitality
to welcome the stranger
at my gate

even you

Letting Loose

Through the door
I see
the red kites rise
soar and swoop
draw my eyes
skywards to the hills
snow capped
sun kissed

grasping my fears
and years
and lethargy
I climb above
gentle fields
fierce forest
through bright gorse
glowing heather

I'm spinning round
letting loose
letting go
absorbed
soaked up
within
red kites
rising

Being Normal

Normal
is how I am today
not yesterday
not tomorrow
just today

normal changes
as dewdrops on petals
as leaves turn and fall
as butterflies rise
or demise

normal is pain
sickness, sleeplessness
sense of detachment
fear
disintegration

but today
my body rests
in a garden of delight
sun's healing warmth
invades my bones
my soul becalmed

tomorrow will be
different
I await the surprises
it will bring

Hope

through the tangle
of wires and words
and weight of worry
I find my way

holding the unknown
close against my heart
hope has arisen
and transformed the day

each moment forms
a precious pearl
to cradle handfast
come what may

Spectacles

I have two pairs

Those glasses are
for reading, writing
practical tasks
they are plain
anonymous
serviceable
light on the nose
easy to lose
amongst the debris
of living
home-birds

These glasses
make a statement
here I am
bright and colourful
spots and swirls
banish the dark
dispel the gloom
attract the eye
the light
glasses-to-go

but through
the lens
the mood creeps
inner turmoil
cold, hunger
worries, distraction
or serenity
peace of mind
changing what's seen
or concealed

choose to imagine
delve beneath
the surface
see beyond
the patina
the camouflage
of people, places
things
ground the feet
breathe
be still

recognise
the hurt, the pain
fear of rejection
faltering step
outreached hand
sideways glance
importunate gaze
be compassionate
mindful
use both glasses
well

Benediction

blessed be the sun in the heavens
for it nurtures all things
to pollinate the earth

blessed be the breeze as it rustles by
for it carries the scent and sound
and hopes of Spring

blessed be the sea, the ebb and flow
for it is my hearth and horizon
borderland to beyond

blessed be my dis-ease
for showering blessings, friendship
love and gifts abounding

blessed be friendship across boundaries
across continents, across the years
for it is as the sun in the heavens

blessed be the healers
who touch me as they pass
for they soothe and season the soul

blessed be time, counting out each precious drop
for each moment is mine to hold
with joy

Rousseau's Tropical Storm With A Tiger

I see this painting
in a picture book
Katie steps into
the frame
the tiger gives chase

I see this painting
in a gallery
so large and bright
colours radiant
the tiger bold

I will not step
into this frame
despite the glory
the vibrancy
of undergrowth

I admire from afar
where it is safe
and teeth and heat
and insects
cannot touch me

For I am timid
in the face
of such luxuriance
such terrifying
boldness

I have my own jungles
to survive
each day

My Life

I am contemplative
alone
a lone survivor
surviving life
complete
content to live

buried deep within me
resources rise
reflecting redemption

I am not lonely
for I am loved
but only I can live this life
entrusted to me
no other
can take my place
bear my pain
experience my pleasure